Dragonheart

Adapted from the junior novelization written by
ADRIANA GABRIEL
Based on the motion picture screenplay written by
CHARLES EDWARD POGUE
Story by
PATRICK READ JOHNSON & CHARLES EDWARD POGUE

Level 2

Retold by Joanna Strange
Series Editors: Andy Hopkins and Jocelyn Potter

Pearson Education Limited
Edinburgh Gate, Harlow,
Essex CM20 2JE, England
and Associated Companies throughout the world.

ISBN 978-0-582-36401-1

First published in Great Britain by Mammoth
an imprint of Reed Children's Books 1996
This edition first published 1999

9 10 8

Typeset by Digital Type, London
Set in 11/14pt Bembo
Printed in China
SWTC/08

Published by Pearson Education Limited in association with
Penguin Books Ltd, both companies being subsidiaries of Pearson Plc

For a complete list of titles available in the Penguin Readers series, please write to your local
Pearson Education office or to: Penguin Readers Marketing Department,
Pearson Education, Edinburgh Gate, Harlow, Essex CM20 2JE.

Contents

Introduction

'I won't be a cruel king. I won't kill dragons and peasants. I'll love my people and be kind to them. I'll always live by the Old Code.'

Young Prince Einon is dying. His mother wants Draco, the Great Dragon, to help him. Draco says that he will help. But first the boy has to repeat these words.

When Einon is king, he forgets the dragon's words. He is cruel to the peasants, and everybody in the country is unhappy and afraid.

Draco and good Sir Bowen, a Knight of the Old Code, want to help the peasants. But can they? Will people live by the Old Code again? What will happen in the fight between Good and Bad?

This story is about dragons and knights, kings and peasants. Charles Edward Pogue wrote the story for the film of *Dragonheart* – a book by Patrick Read Johnson and Charles Edward Pogue. Sean Connery (Draco), Dennis Quaid (Sir Bowen), David Thewlis (Einon), Pete Postlethwaite (Gilbert, the monk) and Julie Christie (Queen Aislinn) are all in the film. It was expensive and difficult to make. They used computers to film the dragon; the beautiful woods, mountains and castles are in Slovakia, in the east of Europe. It is a very exciting film, and a lot of people went to see it at the cinema.

Chapter 1 The Old Code

A sword shone in the sun. 'Not bad!' shouted Sir★ Bowen. Then he pulled out his sword and started to fight Prince Einon. The prince fell to the ground. 'But you'll have to fight harder than that, or you'll die!' laughed Sir Bowen.

Sir Bowen was one of King Freyne's knights. Prince Einon was the king's son. He was fourteen years old and a strong young man. He liked fighting but he didn't like losing. He got up quickly and took up his sword again. 'That's better,' laughed Bowen. The young prince smiled. Then suddenly he felt Bowen's sword, hard, on his arm. 'Dead again!' laughed Sir Bowen.

Einon started to fight again. His face was angry now. 'Careful!

Einon started to fight again. His face was angry now.

★ Sir: important king's knights had the word *Sir* in front of their names.

Careful! Fight with your head, don't fight with your heart, boy!' shouted Bowen.

The knight wanted to make Einon a good fighter. But he also wanted to teach him the Old Code. Sir Bowen and all the kings, princes and knights before him were Knights of the Old Code. For thousands of years kings were kind to peasants and knights helped kings. This was the Old Code. Life was good, and everybody in the country was happy. Then everything started to change and the peasants were angry. Bowen didn't like this. He loved Einon and he wanted the boy to remember the Old Code all his life.

After the sword-fighting lesson, Bowen and Einon sat down. 'Never turn your back to somebody when you fight, Einon! Why can't you remember that?'

Suddenly they heard the sound of a horse. They looked up and saw Brok, one of the king's knights, on his horse in front of them. Bowen didn't like Brok and looked at him angrily. Brok didn't live by the Old Code.

'We're fighting the peasants,' Brok told them. 'We're winning, of course. King Freyne wants his son to come and watch.'

'It's not good or clever to fight the peasants,' answered Bowen. He really hated Brok.

'They're stupid! The king says they have to die. He wants Einon to come now. And you too, Bowen,' Brok shouted. Then he turned his horse and rode away fast.

'Why did he shout at you?' asked Einon. 'You're a Knight of the Old Code! You're not afraid of him!'

'No, of course I'm not afraid of him. I hate him. He doesn't live by the Old Code. He enjoys killing the peasants. He's the king's man.'

Einon understood. Bowen hated his father, the king, too. He smiled at Bowen. 'When my father dies, I'll be king. And you'll be my man, Sir Bowen.'

Bowen looked at Einon with love in his eyes. 'I'm your man *now*, my Prince,' he answered warmly.

Chapter 2   The Battle

Brok rode quickly back to the battle. When he got near the fighting, he heard the sound of swords. He laughed loudly when he saw hundreds of peasants, dead on the ground.

In the middle of a field, Brok could see King Freyne on his horse. The crown on the king's head shone in the sun. On his coat was a picture of a dragon's head on a sword. The king looked down at the dead men below him with hard eyes. With a cruel smile on his face, he pulled out his sword. The peasants on his right and left were afraid. They ran away fast but the king followed them. He loved fighting and killing. Nothing could stop him now.

High above the battle, Sir Bowen and Prince Einon sat and watched. Bowen hated the fighting but Einon was excited.

'I want to fight down there with my father,' he said.

'No, you don't, boy,' Bowen answered sadly.

'I do! I do!' Einon shouted. 'And I want to see you fight too, Sir Bowen. You're the best fighter in the world!'

'Yes, I *am* a good fighter. Better than your cruel father,' Bowen said angrily.

Einon felt unhappy when he heard this. 'Don't be angry with him, Bowen. He *is* my father and he *is* the king.'

Bowen smiled kindly at the prince. He didn't want to make Einon unhappy. But it was difficult for him to watch the battle. He was a Knight of the Old Code, and it was wrong to kill the peasants.

'Yes, Einon, your father's king now,' he said to the boy. 'But one day you'll be king and you'll wear the crown on your head. When you're king, remember today. And remember the Old

Code. Never, never fight the peasants. Then the crown will shine wonderfully on your head, and you'll be a better king than your father.'

Bowen turned to watch the battle with a heavy heart. He didn't see the prince's eyes when Einon spoke. They were as hard as the king's.

'Yes, I'm going to be a better king than my father, Bowen,' answered Einon. Then he suddenly shouted, 'Oh, look! My father's killing more stupid peasants!'

Down below them, the king and his knights rode through the peasants' village. They cut down men with their swords and burnt their homes. One of the peasants stood near his house and watched the king carefully. This man's name was Redbeard – he had red hair and a red beard. He suddenly shouted loudly, 'Now!'

When the other men heard Redbeard, they quickly came out of their houses. They looked angry and dangerous. They ran after Redbeard to the king on his horse and tried to kill him. The king rode out of the village fast, but the peasants followed him. They pulled him from his horse and began to hit him. Then they all jumped on him, hard.

From above, Einon watched the fighting and cried, 'No! No! They're killing my father!' He quickly jumped on his horse and rode down to the battle.

'Stop, Einon! Stop!' shouted Bowen, but Einon didn't listen. Bowen climbed on to his horse and followed fast behind the boy. But when he got to the battle, he couldn't find the prince anywhere. 'Einon! Einon!' he called, but there was no answer.

Einon found his father on the ground and sat down near him. He looked at the king's grey face and cried, 'Father, father!'

Then he looked at the beautiful crown on the king's head. 'My father's going to die,' he thought. 'I'm going to be king and I want that crown now.'

Einon started to take the crown from his father's head, but the king suddenly opened his eyes. He looked at the boy and tried to stop him. For a minute, father and son pulled at the crown. But Einon was stronger and he won. Old King Freyne looked at his son angrily. Then he closed his eyes and died.

When Einon stood up with the crown in his hands, he saw a young peasant opposite him. The man stood on a bridge with a large bucket on his head! He suddenly jumped off the bridge and fell on to Einon. They fought for a long time. Then the peasant, Buckethead, pushed his sword into Einon's heart. The prince fell to the ground with his hands round the crown.

When the peasant looked down at the prince at his feet, the bucket fell from his head. Einon could see a lot of lovely, long red hair! Buckethead was a woman, not a man. Her name was Kara, and she was Redbeard's daughter. She wore dirty, old clothes but she was very beautiful.

Suddenly somebody shouted, 'Einon, Einon! Where are you?' When Kara heard this, she quickly ran away. Sir Bowen ran to Einon and cried, 'It's me, Einon. I'm here, My King.'

Einon looked up at Bowen, and then closed his eyes. Bowen took the prince in his arms and tried to help him. But the boy didn't move. The knight could do nothing.

Chapter 3   The Great Dragon

In the king's castle, Queen Aislinn sat in her room. She looked out of the window with sad eyes. She couldn't see the battle, but she could hear the sound of fighting. 'The Old Code says it's wrong to kill the peasants,' she thought. 'My husband's a bad, cruel king.'

Suddenly Brok, the king's knight, ran into the room. 'Queen Aislinn, your husband's dead,' he said. 'The peasants killed him. King Freyne is dead!'

The queen listened to Brok quietly. Behind him she could see

The queen stood next to Bowen and looked down at her son.

Sir Bowen. His face was tired and sad and he stood with her son, Prince Einon, in his arms.

'I'm sorry, Queen Aislinn,' said Bowen, with his head down. 'The prince fell too.'

'Don't be sorry, Sir Bowen,' answered the queen. 'They killed Einon because of his cruel father, the king. Now, put him on my bed.'

But Einon wasn't dead. 'The crown, the crown ...,' he said weakly. Bowen put the crown into Einon's hands. But the queen didn't listen to him. She stood next to Bowen and looked down at her son. Then she slowly took off his shirt.

'We can't help him now,' Bowen said sadly.

The queen said nothing. She walked to the window and looked at a beautiful picture of a dragon on the wall. 'Perhaps we can, Bowen,' she answered. 'Perhaps we can ...'

◆

Queen Aislinn rode quickly. She turned her horse and started to climb the mountain behind the castle. Brok rode in front of her and Sir Bowen followed. Behind them two men carried Einon carefully up the mountain.

After a long time, Bowen heard the sound of music – a strange, sad song. It came from somewhere inside the mountain. Then Einon made a sound and his eyes closed. Bowen got off his horse fast and ran to the young boy. 'Wake up! Wake up!' he shouted. 'Don't go to sleep, My King. You can't die now. Listen to me, and remember the Old Code.' Bowen then spoke quietly into Einon's ear. He talked to him about the Old Code. Einon moved his mouth and tried to repeat Bowen's words. He didn't want to die on the cold mountain.

They climbed slowly up the mountain, then stopped. The queen got off her horse and turned to the men behind her.

'This is the end of our journey. We're going into the mountain now.'

It was a cold, dark place and it looked dangerous.

'Follow me. Don't be afraid,' said the queen. She walked in and the men followed her. They couldn't see much. There was a lot of smoke, and there were dead animals on the ground near their feet. Then Bowen heard the strange song again.

Suddenly, the music stopped. From out of the dark somebody asked sadly, 'Are the stars shining tonight?'

'No, there aren't any stars in the sky tonight,' answered the queen.

'Is that Queen Aislinn, wife of King Freyne?' said the dragon.

'Yes, Great Dragon. The people in my country love you and the other dragons. We're your friends.'

'No, Madam,' answered the dragon. 'Men and dragons were friends for thousands of years. But things are different now.'

The dragon came slowly out of the dark and sat on the ground near the queen.

'Bring Einon here, Bowen,' said the queen.

The knight carried Einon in his arms and put him down on the ground. The dragon's face was high above him. It was very ugly – brown and black, with a large mouth, big teeth, and sad eyes. Bowen felt very afraid – he never took his eyes away from that face!

The dragon looked down at Einon. 'It's King Freyne's son!' he said. 'I hated the king. He loved killing dragons and peasants. What do you want from me, Queen Aislinn?'

'I want your help,' answered the queen. 'A peasant hurt my child in the battle. Einon's not the same as his father, Great Dragon. This knight, Sir Bowen, is teaching him the Old Code. And I'm going to teach him about dragons in the future. Please help him.'

'You're asking a lot, Madam. Your son's very ill,' said the dragon.

The dragon's face was high above Bowen.

'I know,' cried the queen. 'But he's king now. He'll be a good king. Sir Bowen and I will help him. He won't be cruel, Great Dragon.'

'*He* has to say that, not *you*,' answered the dragon. Then he looked at Bowen. 'Give me your sword, Knight.'

Bowen pulled out his sword and gave it to the dragon. The dragon stood over Einon, with the sword in his hands. The boy opened his eyes. He saw the dragon, and tried to move away.

'Don't be afraid, son,' said the queen quietly. 'The Great Dragon's going to help you.'

'I *will* help you, boy. But first you have to say these words: "I won't be a cruel king. I won't kill dragons and peasants. I'll love my people and be kind to them. I'll always live by the Old Code." Now, are you ready? Repeat them after me!'

Einon was very tired, but he repeated the dragon's words. Then he fell back into Bowen's arms.

'Einon, Einon!' shouted Bowen. 'No, no! He's dead!' Bowen was very angry and tried to pull his sword away from the dragon.

But the dragon shouted, 'Knight of the Old Code. Stop! Watch me! Now!' Then he pushed Bowen's sword into his heart! A red light came out of the dragon. He caught the light in his hands and turned to Einon. 'This light's half my heart, boy. I'm giving it to you. It'll make you strong. Enjoy a long life and always remember the words of the Old Code.'

Einon's eyes slowly opened. He felt weak, but he wasn't dead. Bowen looked at the boy, then he looked up at the dragon. 'I'm sorry, Great Dragon. I was angry and afraid. Thank you.'

'You can help Einon now, Sir Bowen. Teach him the Old Code well. Never forget my words.'

Before Bowen could answer, the dragon went back into the mountain. Everything was dark and cold again. Nobody spoke – they listened to the sound of the strange, sad music.

Chapter 4   Cruel King Einon

Einon sat on his horse, high above the peasants. He looked strong and happy with his father's crown on his head and his sword in his hand.

'*I'm* king now,' he thought. 'I love watching my peasants. They're building me a wonderful new castle. It's going to be bigger and better than my father's old castle. It's going to be the greatest castle in the world!'

King Einon was as hard and cruel as his father now. He never remembered the words of the Old Code, or the Great Dragon in the mountain. He hated the peasants, and they had to work harder and harder every day.

Brok, old King Freyne's knight, rode past Einon on his horse. Behind Brok, some peasants walked slowly up to the castle. They looked weak and ill. They didn't look up at the king when they walked past. But Einon looked down at them and suddenly shouted loudly, 'Stop, Brok! Stop!'

Brok quickly jumped down from his horse.

'Look, Brok! There! That peasant there! That's Redbeard! He killed my father!'

Einon and Brok looked at the tall, strong peasant with the red hair and red beard. Redbeard looked back at them with hate in his eyes.

'Yes, I killed your father, boy!' he shouted at Einon. 'You can thank me now. Now you're king and the crown's on your head.'

Brok ran to Redbeard and put his sword up near his face.

'No!' Einon shouted. 'Don't kill him. That's too kind.' He smiled cruelly at Redbeard. 'Look at me, dog! Look carefully. You can see me now, but you'll never see me or anything again. Get some wood from the fire, Brok. Burn out his eyes!'

Brok got some wood from a hot fire. Redbeard watched him

angrily but he wasn't afraid. Brok put the burning wood near Redbeard's eyes, then he suddenly stopped. He felt a sword on his arm, and the wood fell from his hands to the ground. He looked up quickly and saw Sir Bowen. Bowen called to the peasants, 'Run away! Quickly! Run!' The peasants understood. They ran away from King Einon and his castle as fast as they could.

Kara, Redbeard's beautiful daughter, ran to her father. 'Father! Father! Are you all right?' she cried.

'Kara! Quickly!' shouted Redbeard. 'Let's go. Run!' And Redbeard and Kara followed the other peasants.

King Einon was very angry with Bowen. He jumped down from his horse and pulled out his sword. 'What are you doing, Bowen?' he shouted angrily. 'Those are *my* peasants, not *yours*! Who's king in this country? Me! Not you!'

Bowen got off his horse and pulled out his sword too. They started to fight, but after a few minutes Einon fell to the ground. Bowen stood over the boy and looked down at him.

'Einon,' he said, 'don't do this. What's wrong with you? Are you ill? Remember the Old Code, Einon. Remember my words and the words of the Great Dragon.'

'I'm king now,' Einon shouted back. 'Kings don't have to live by the Old Code!'

Bowen couldn't understand Einon. He took him by the arm and cried, 'I taught you the Old Code, boy. I taught you everything. Never forget that. What's wrong with you?'

But Einon didn't listen. He pulled his arm away and started to fight Bowen again. Again he fell to the ground. Bowen looked down at him sadly. 'Fight with your head, boy!' he said. 'Don't fight with your heart!'

His heart! His heart! Bowen thought about the dragon's words in the mountain: 'This light's half my heart, boy. I'm giving it to you.' Why was Einon as cruel as his father now? Was it because he had a dragon's heart, not a man's heart? Bowen threw his sword down on the ground next to Einon. He sat down near him on the ground and looked into his eyes.

'Everybody has to live by the Old Code, Einon. Kings, knights and peasants – everybody in the country. Why can't you understand that?' Then he slowly stood up. He got on his horse, and rode away.

Brok wanted to ride after Bowen, but King Einon said, 'Let him go, Brok. He's an old man. He doesn't understand. I don't want him to help me now. I'm a king, not a child. Go and find Redbeard. And when you find him, burn out the stupid peasant's eyes!'

Brok rode away fast and looked for Redbeard. When he found him, he burnt out his eyes, slowly and cruelly. The peasant could never see Kara, his beautiful daughter, again.

♦

Bowen slowly rode away from Einon with a heavy heart. He thought hard about the boy and the dragon. 'Einon isn't a cruel boy. But he's got half the dragon's heart. That's the problem. It's the dragon's heart. So now he's as bad as his father. I'm going to find that dragon . . . and kill him!'

The knight rode quickly back to Queen Aislinn's castle. Then he started on his long journey to find the dragon.

After many days he arrived at the dragon's cold, dark home in the mountain. But this time the dragon wasn't there.

Bowen shouted loudly, 'Dragon! Can you hear me? Where are you, Dragon? Why did you do it? Why did you give my King half your cruel heart? I'll never stop looking for you, Dragon. And when I find you . . .'

Bowen stopped shouting. He stood in the dark and listened. Outside, from somewhere above him, he could hear the dragon's strange song. He quickly jumped on his horse and rode away. He wanted to find the music . . . and the dragon.

Chapter 5   Sir Bowen and the Dragon

Sir Bowen rode up the mountain all day and all night. Early the next morning he saw an old man on the road in front of him.

'Who's this?' he thought. 'Who's he talking to? And why is he riding a horse and writing at the same time?'

'Old man!' he shouted. 'Be careful! Look at the road, not at your books. Now please, move out of my way.'

The old man turned round and saw Bowen. Then suddenly his face went white. He looked very afraid. 'No! Help! There's a dra ... dra ... drag ...'

'What is it?' asked Bowen. 'What's wrong?'

'Be ... be ... behind you,' answered the old man. 'Look behind you!'

Bowen turned round quickly. Behind him there was a big, ugly dragon in the sky! The knight pulled out his sword and they began to fight. This dragon wasn't as big or strong as the Great Dragon in the mountain. In minutes it fell to the ground with Bowen's sword in its heart. Then everything went very quiet.

The old man spoke first. 'Oh, thank you, thank you, Knight! That dragon looked very dangerous. We nearly died! I'd like to thank you a thousand times!'

'All right, all right, it's dead now,' answered Bowen. 'Old man, what's your name? And what are you doing here?'

'My name's Brother Gilbert, and I'm a monk. I ride on my horse round the country and try to help people. And I write stories about my journeys. I write about kings and knights, about dragons and the Old Code.'

'Well, I'm on a long journey too, Brother. So I'll say goodbye now,' answered Bowen.

'Will you ride with me, Knight? asked Brother Gilbert.

'Yes, I'd like to ride with you, Brother. We can talk. Let's go.'

And the two men went slowly up the mountain.

When it was dark, they stopped for the night. They were hungry and thirsty, and they cooked some meat on a hot fire. Then the monk read one of his stories to Bowen. It was a story about the Old Code.

'What do you think, Sir Bowen? Did you like it?' asked Brother Gilbert at the end.

'I liked the meat, Brother, but not your story. The Old Code's dead,' said Bowen sadly. 'Nobody lives by the Old Code now.'

'Ride with me, good Knight, and find the Old Code again,' answered Brother Gilbert.

'I'll ride with you, Brother. But I'm not going to look for the Old Code. I'm looking for a dragon. And when I find it, I'm going to kill it!'

The next morning Bowen and Brother Gilbert climbed on their horses again. They talked and laughed. The monk told Bowen more stories. After some time, Gilbert got off his horse and sat down on the ground. He started to write a story about Bowen and the dragon. Suddenly the ground round the monk began to move and his pen fell out of his fingers. Then his papers flew everywhere.

'Help! Help! What's happening?' he shouted.

Bowen turned round on his horse and saw the monk with his papers on the ground. Then, in the river behind him, he saw a dragon! He rode quickly down to the river. When he got there, he heard the dragon's strange song again.

'Don't come into this river, Knight, or you'll die!' the dragon said.

'I'm not afraid of you,' shouted Bowen.

'Aren't you?' shouted the dragon. 'Then look at this!'

Out of the river the dragon threw a dead man and his horse. 'That man tried to follow me into the river! Look at him now! And there are more down here!'

Brother Gilbert stood behind Bowen. He was very afraid. But

the knight got off his horse and pulled out his sword. 'Come and fight me, Dragon,' he shouted. 'You can't hurt me.'

The dragon came slowly out of the river and went behind a tree. Bowen could feel the hot fire from the dragon's nose, but he couldn't see him very well. On the ground, round the tree, were dead men and horses.

Bowen moved nearer the tree. He felt afraid, but he didn't want the dragon to know. 'Why is all that fire coming out of your nose, Dragon? It's too wet in the river to start a fire, you know!' he laughed.

'Why do you knights always want to fight and kill us? Do you think it'll make you famous?' the dragon asked.

'I don't want to be famous,' answered Bowen, with his sword in his hand. 'But I want to be rich. These days people pay me for dead dragons. And I'm going to kill you.'

'Oh, you kill dragons for money! You're *that* knight!' said the dragon.

'Well, I have to live,' answered Bowen.

'Yes, everybody has to live,' laughed the dragon. 'Let's start the battle then.'

'Yes, let's,' shouted Bowen. 'I'll enjoy killing you!'

Bowen moved nearer. The dragon watched him and then he saw the knight's sword. 'I know that sword,' he thought. 'I used it in the mountain to cut out half my heart for King Einon.' He suddenly left the ground and flew up into the sky. He flew higher and higher, above Sir Bowen and Brother Gilbert.

The knight quickly climbed on to his horse and rode after the dragon. Bowen followed him for a long time but in the end he got down from his horse, tired and angry. Then the dragon flew down from the sky.

'You're clever,' shouted Bowen. 'Cleverer than the other dragons. Come here! I want a good fight.'

'Well, it'll be your last,' said the dragon.

They started to fight. The dragon hit Bowen hard and he fell back into a tree. He got up quickly and shouted, 'You won't win, you know. I'm going to kill all dragons.'

'There's only me, Knight. I'm the last dragon.'

Bowen didn't know that this was the last dragon in the country. When he heard this, he stopped fighting for a minute. The dragon watched him and came nearer. He pushed Bowen hard and the knight fell over. Bowen could feel the fire from the dragon's nose. It burnt his face. He heard Brother Gilbert shout. Then everything went black . . .

♦

When Bowen woke up, he was inside the dragon's mouth. He pulled out his sword and shouted, 'Don't bring your teeth down, Dragon. Or my sword will go up.' Nothing happened.

Bowen sat in the dragon's mouth all day. Outside, Brother Gilbert watched and waited. In the evening the dragon tried to speak, but it was difficult with Bowen in his mouth!

'Don't put your sword ufp. Or ma teef come down,' he said.

Bowen looked round the dragon's mouth. He saw an old shirt between two of the dragon's teeth. He pulled it out and a man's hand came out with it. 'Oh, that's Sir Eglamore's shirt!' he cried, and threw it away.

'Thannffs!' said the dragon. 'That's been ufp dere fa monffs! Now ged your sword off ma teef.'

'Oh be quiet! It's hard for me too, you know,' answered Bowen.

The conversation was very boring and difficult for the dragon. 'Oh, ma mouf if dry,' said the dragon after a short time. 'Listen, ged out aff ma mouf and led's talk face to face.'

Bowen got up slowly and the dragon opened his mouth. The knight stood between his big, dirty teeth. With his sword in his

The knight stood between the dragon's big, dirty teeth.

hands, he looked up at the dragon – he felt very afraid. Then he suddenly fell on to the ground outside with his sword next to him.

'Kill me, then!' he shouted up to the dragon.

'I don't want to kill you,' said the dragon quietly. 'And I don't want you to kill me. I'm old and tired and I don't want to fight. I've got an idea. Listen.'

Bowen was tired and hungry. He wanted to eat and sleep. He looked up at the dragon and said weakly, 'So tell me. What's your idea?'

Chapter 6   The Dragon's Idea

The dragon began to tell Bowen his clever idea.

At the same time, down below them, the peasants worked hard in Sir Felton's fields. Sir Felton was one of King Einon's rich knights.

One of the boys suddenly stopped his work and looked up at the sky. 'Father, father!' he cried. 'Look! Up there!' The peasants looked at the boy. Then they looked up at the sky. There, above them, was the dragon!

'Help! He's coming down!' they shouted. 'Look at that fire! It's coming out of his nose! It's going to burn us! Run! Fast!'

The dragon flew down to the ground. He started to burn down Sir Felton's fields and buildings – there was fire and smoke everywhere. Sir Felton heard the peasants and quickly ran out of his house. But before he could say a word, somebody behind him said, 'Look at that! Those dragons! Can I help?'

Sir Felton was very, very angry. He looked round and saw Sir Bowen with a smile on his face. 'Stupid dragon!' he shouted. 'Look! My fields! And my buildings! They're burning!'

'Well, I can help you,' answered Bowen. 'But you'll have to pay me – it'll cost a lot of money.'

'I won't pay you anything,' shouted back Sir Felton. 'Do you hear me?'

He turned and started to go back into his house. But the house was also on fire. 'No, no! Not my house too! Don't burn my beautiful house! Help!' Sir Felton cried. And he ran back to Bowen fast. 'Here. Take this money. Quickly. Do something.'

Minutes later, Bowen and the peasants were ready. When the dragon flew over them, they started to throw things at him. This was the dragon's wonderful idea! He cried, 'Oh ... oh ... oh!' Then he slowly fell down from the sky and into a river near Sir Felton's house.

'He's dying! He's dying!' shouted the peasants. 'Look, he's in the river!' They all laughed happily, but Sir Felton looked very angry.

'Get my money back,' he shouted at them. 'Run after that knight. He's got my money.' The peasants ran after Sir Bowen as fast as they could.

Bowen didn't wait. He quickly jumped on to his horse near the river and rode away. With Sir Felton's money in his hand, he laughed loudly. 'We did it! It was easy! Clever dragon!' He looked down at the money. 'Now let's see. How much have we got?'

A long way down the river, the dragon's head came up out of the water. He swam round and round and waited for Sir Bowen. When the knight saw him, he called, 'Well, Dragon, your idea was wonderful! They think you're dead. And we made a lot of money.'

'There's a lot of money in the world, Knight,' answered the dragon sadly. 'You'll find it all, and then you won't want me.'

'No, Dragon,' answered Bowen. 'I'm a Knight of the Old Code. I'll never forget you.'

The dragon swam round in the river. He looked up at the knight on his horse. 'You've got Sir Felton's money. But do you feel bad now?' he asked. 'You didn't really kill me.'

Bowen looked down at the dragon. 'No, I don't feel bad. Sir Felton doesn't live by the Old Code – he's cruel to the peasants.'

'Yes, but when you took his money, he was angry. And he'll be angry with the peasants now. They'll have to work harder and harder. And he won't pay them a penny,' answered the dragon.

'That's not my problem,' shouted Bowen. 'You don't understand the Old Code. You're only a dragon!'

'All right, don't be angry, Knight,' said the dragon quietly. 'I *do* know about the Old Code. And I know you tried to live by it.'

'Yes, but nobody wanted to listen to me. So now I'm not going to try,' answered Bowen sadly. 'I can't change the world, Dragon.'

The dragon's eyes were as sad and tired as Bowen's. They started moving down the river again.

When evening came, the dragon and Bowen stopped for dinner. They were near cruel King Einon's castle. Bowen was hungry and ate quickly.

The dragon waited and then asked, 'Why do you hate dragons, Knight?'

'I don't hate *all* dragons,' Bowen answered. 'I hate one dragon and I wanted to kill him. But I never found him. And now I'll never find him. You're the last dragon, so he's dead.'

'Tell me,' said the dragon quietly, 'why did you hate that dragon?'

'He only had half a heart,' Bowen answered. 'He gave the other half to King Einon. But it made Einon cruel and bad. When he had the dragon's heart, he forgot the Old Code. He killed peasants and he was as cruel as his father, King Freyne.'

The dragon listened and he began to look very angry. 'Einon was bad before he met that dragon,' he shouted. 'He was cruel before he got half the dragon's heart.'

Bowen stood up quickly. 'How do you know that?' he asked.

The dragon knew because *he* was the Great Dragon in the

The dragon waited and then asked, 'Why do you hate dragons, Knight?'

mountain. He gave Einon half his heart. But he didn't want to discuss that with Bowen. 'Well . . . um . . . all dragons know that,' he said. 'They know that Einon was a cruel child. And now he's a cruel king.'

Bowen didn't like this. The dragon's words made him unhappy. 'No! I knew Einon when he was little! He was a good boy. I taught him the Old Code,' he cried.

'Then he was cruel to you too,' said the dragon. He stood nose-to-nose with Bowen. 'He broke your heart. And he broke the kind dragon's heart too.'

'No, Dragon, he didn't,' shouted Sir Bowen.

'Oh, stop calling me "dragon"! I've got a name, you know!'

'What is it then, Dragon?' asked Bowen.

'Well, uh, I can't say it in your language,' answered the dragon.

21

'Go on. Try,' said Bowen.

'Arr . . . er . . . awrr . . . ow-w-wsh-s . . .'

'You're right,' laughed Bowen. 'I can't say that.'

He turned to put some more wood on the fire. With his back to the dragon, he suddenly heard a sad sound. He turned and saw the dragon on the ground.

'Aah. It hurts,' said the dragon. He closed his eyes and put his hand on his heart. Bowen could see a red light near the dragon's heart. He quickly put some water on the light, and the dragon slowly opened his eyes.

'Thank you. I'm all right now,' he said.

'What was it?' asked Bowen.

'Oh nothing. I had a bad accident once, and it hurts sometimes.'

'I hope our conversation didn't make you unhappy,' said Bowen.

'It wasn't you,' said the dragon. 'Not you . . .'

That night Bowen sat next to the dragon for a long time. He watched the red light near the dragon's heart. The colour got slowly weaker and weaker. In the middle of the night the dragon opened his eyes.

'Why aren't you asleep?' he asked, when he saw Bowen.

'I didn't want to sleep. I wanted to think of a name for you,' answered Bowen. 'And I found a name. Up there. Can you see those stars?'

The dragon looked up at the sky. 'Yes,' he said.

'We call those stars Draco,' said Bowen. 'In our language, "draco" is the same as "dragon".'

'And would you like to call me Draco?' laughed the dragon.

'No, you're right. It's a stupid idea,' said Bowen, with his head down.

'No,' said the dragon kindly. 'It's not stupid. I like the name Draco. Thank you, Knight. And have you got a name?'

'Yes, my name's Bowen.'

'Thank you, Bowen,' said Draco, and he put his arm round the knight.

Chapter 7   A Sad Day for Kara

King Einon sat on his horse and looked at his new castle. 'Good. The peasants are working hard,' he thought. 'I was right. This is going to be the biggest and most beautiful castle in the world.'

Below him, the peasants worked hard in the hot sun. They were all hungry and thirsty but they couldn't stop work. Kara, Redbeard's beautiful daughter, walked round with a large bucket of water. She gave the men a drink when she spoke to them. She wore old, dark clothes, but she looked lovely with her long, red hair and kind face. Kara went to an old man. It was her father, Redbeard. His hair and beard were grey now. He wore old clothes too, and his hands and arms were dirty.

'Drink, father,' Kara said. She looked at her father's eyes. 'Cruel King Einon burnt your eyes, dear father, but you have to eat and drink.'

'Kara! Don't come here. It's dangerous. Please go home!' said the old man, when he heard his daughter.

'No, father. I'm not listening to you. Drink!' Kara said.

The old man put his hand up to her face. 'You're not a child now. You're a woman, a beautiful woman,' Redbeard said. 'One day the king or one of his knights will see you. And they'll want you. Go home, Kara!'

'You're my home, father,' answered Kara. 'Now drink this.' And she gave the old man a cup of water.

Suddenly a sword pushed the cup out of Redbeard's hand. Kara looked up. In front of her she saw Einon and his knights on their horses.

'Don't move, father,' said Kara quietly.

'That was clever, King Einon,' laughed Sir Felton. 'Now try the water bucket. There. Behind the stupid old peasant!'

Einon laughed and pushed the bucket with his sword. The water went over Redbeard.

'Don't move, father,' said Kara quietly.

She left her father and went to King Einon and Sir Felton. The knight threw his sword down hard at Kara's feet, but she wasn't afraid.

'Look at the girl!' shouted Einon. 'What are you doing?'

'My father's an old man, King Einon,' Kara cried. 'He can't fight you now. Please, don't hurt him.'

'Don't hurt him?' Einon shouted, and quickly moved nearer Redbeard. Then he pushed his sword hard into the peasant's heart.

'Father!' shouted Kara and ran to the old man on the ground.

Einon watched and smiled. 'Your father's dead!' he laughed.

Kara had Redbeard in her arms. Her beautiful, long red hair fell down her back. Einon looked at her. He remembered the girl's lovely hair, but not her name. 'Who is she?' he thought. 'She's beautiful. What's her name? Where does she come from?' Then he turned his horse and started to ride away.

Kara looked down at her father, dead in her arms. Then she looked up at Einon and his knights on their horses. 'I hate that cruel man,' she said quietly. 'He killed my father. I'll never forget that. One day . . .'

Chapter 8   Kara Meets Draco

At his castle King Einon sat down to dinner. His knights and their wives ate with him. At the end of the table his mother, Queen Aislinn, sat quietly. The other men and women at the table were loud and noisy.

Suddenly Einon turned round. He saw somebody behind him with a knife in his hand. The man threw the knife at the king, but he was ready. Einon caught him and pushed him down on to the table. Then Einon and Brok, the king's cruel knight, looked down at the man. But it wasn't a man! It was a woman! She had beautiful, long red hair. It was Kara!

'I know you,' Einon said. 'You're Redbeard's child.' Then he turned to Queen Aislinn. 'Look at her, Mother! She tried to kill me!'

The queen looked at her son, but she didn't say a word. Einon looked at Kara. 'I killed your father, girl,' he said to her. 'And now I'm going to kill you.'

'Kill me then! I want to die,' shouted Kara. 'I don't want to live in this country. You're not my king!'

'So what shall I do with you? I'll think of something,' Einon shouted at her. 'Now, take her away!'

She had beautiful, long red hair. It was Kara!

Brok and some other knights quickly took Kara out of the room.

Einon looked down at her knife in his hands, and then he looked at his mother. The queen watched him but she said nothing. Einon threw the knife down on the table and looked into the hot fire. He thought for a minute. Then he suddenly stood up and ran out of the room.

'Where is she? Where's that woman?' he shouted. He found Kara in a small dark room in the bottom of the castle. 'I remember you now!' Einon shouted at her. 'Your red hair! At the battle! When my father, the king, died! It was your sword! It went through my heart!' He opened his shirt. 'Look! *You* did that. Now *I'll* find a way to hurt *you.*'

Kara looked into Einon's eyes. She wasn't afraid. 'Next time I'll kill you!' she shouted at him.

'You can't. I've got a different heart now. It's very strong,' answered Einon.

'Your heart's black,' Kara shouted.

When he heard this, Einon looked at her with cruel eyes. 'You wait,' he said. 'I'll think of something . . .'

Kara sat in the cold room and looked out of the small window. How could she get out? But then Queen Aislinn came quietly into the room.

'You!' Kara said. 'How did you get in here?'

'Ssh! Be quiet! I want to help you,' said the queen.

'I don't want any help from the mother of that cruel king,' answered Kara.

'I *am* Einon's mother,' the queen said sadly. 'But he had a father too. I had to marry King Freyne, but I didn't want to be his wife. Einon's cruel because of his father, not me.'

'Why didn't you kill him when he was a baby then?' shouted Kara.

'You can ask that now,' the queen answered. 'But when a mother looks at the baby in her arms, she only sees her child. She doesn't know that he's going to be a cruel man.'

'And now you want to help me,' Kara said. 'All right. Give me my knife. Then I can die.'

'Don't die now, my girl, when you can live,' said the queen. Then she showed Kara a small door behind the fireplace. 'Only three people know about this door,' she said. She opened it and quickly walked outside the castle walls with Kara. 'Can you see that road?' the queen asked. 'Run away now. Run fast!'

Kara turned to say thank you to Queen Aislinn, but she wasn't there!

◆

'What? Dogs!' shouted Einon angrily. 'Stupid men! Where's the girl? How did she get out?' Einon threw his food and drink on the floor. Brok and Queen Aislinn watched him.

'Sir, there's only one way out of that room,' Brok said. 'And only you, me and the queen know about it.'

'I know!' shouted Einon. 'So how did the girl find the door?' His eyes turned to his mother. 'It was her,' he thought. 'She helped her.'

He shouted at Brok, 'Get your best men. Quickly. Go and find her. And bring her here fast.'

Brok ran out, and the queen said quietly to her son, 'I'll ask somebody to clean up this room.' Einon looked at his mother with cold, angry eyes.

Kara ran away from the castle as fast as she could. When she arrived at her village, she told everybody her story. 'I've got a plan to kill the king. Will you help me?' she asked the villagers. But they were afraid. They didn't want to hear her ideas. Her father, Redbeard, was dead. They didn't want to die too. 'Listen to me! We have to fight!' said Kara. But the men shouted at her and started to hit her.

'Stop that!' somebody behind them said. They turned and saw Sir Bowen on his horse. Then suddenly one of the men cried, 'Look! Look up there!' It was Draco, the dragon, high in the sky!

'You're late!' thought Bowen, when he saw the dragon.

Draco flew down near the village. 'Look at that fire!' the men shouted. 'It's coming out of his nose! He's going to burn our village!' Some of the villagers ran away into their houses, but Kara and the oldest man in the village stayed behind.

'Do you want me to kill this dragon?' Bowen asked them. 'You'll have to pay me, or I'll leave him here!'

Kara looked very angry. 'I thought King Einon was cruel. But this knight is worse,' she said to the old man. 'Don't give him our money.'

Bowen looked hard at Kara and said to the old man, 'All right. Don't give me any money. But why don't you give the dragon one of the village's lovely young women? Then he'll go away.'

The other men came out of their houses and listened to Bowen. Then they all looked at Kara. 'Yes, give *her* to the dragon,' they shouted.

'Who's that girl?' asked Draco.

'The villagers want you to have her. Then you'll go away,' answered Bowen.

'That's stupid! Who gave them that idea?' Draco laughed.

'I don't know,' Bowen said quietly. 'What are you waiting for? Quickly. Go and eat her!'

'Oh, please!' said Draco. 'I feel ill. Yech!'

'But you ate Sir Eglamore. I saw him when I was in your mouth,' said Bowen. 'Think of something. Quickly!'

Draco put out his arms and pulled Kara away from the men in the village. Then he flew away with her into the sky. Everybody shouted and laughed. They were very happy.

'Thank you, Knight. Thank you. Now we'll never see Kara or the dragon again!'

Chapter 9   Ready for Battle

'That's lovely, Draco.' Kara sat in the hot sun with a smile on her face. Draco sat next to her and sang his sad, strange song. 'And you're a lovely dragon. They're not all as kind as you are,' said Kara. She felt warm and happy.

'How many dragons do you know then?' Draco asked.

'You're the first,' answered Kara. 'But you're funny. You don't eat young women – you sing to them! Do you do anything dangerous?'

'No,' said Draco. 'When people are kind to me, I never hurt them.'

'Then why did you come to my village?' asked Kara.

'Good question!' said somebody behind them. It was Bowen. 'You remember Kara's village, Draco. Why did you go there?'

Kara looked angrily at Bowen. 'Go away, Knight,' she shouted. 'You wanted this dragon to eat me!' Then she got up and tried to fight Bowen.

They fell into the river and Bowen shouted out, 'Help! Draco, why *didn't* you eat her?'

Draco smiled and answered, 'Kara, this is Sir Bowen. He won't hurt you. Bowen meet Kara.'

Kara and Bowen stopped fighting and got out of the river. But before they could say anything, they heard the sound of horses. Draco heard them too and quickly jumped into the water.

Einon, Brok and the king's other knights came out of the trees. Bowen ran in front of Kara – he didn't want them to see her. Kara looked at Bowen and suddenly remembered his face. 'He helped my father,' she thought. 'When I was younger and Einon tried to burn out his eyes the first time. He was a good Knight of the Old Code then. Why is he different now?' But she didn't have time to think about that. Einon sat above her on his horse. He looked down at the girl and the knight.

'Ah, my old teacher!' he said cruelly. 'And you've got my woman. I lost her. But here she is!'

'I don't think she's *your* woman, King Einon. She doesn't want to come with you,' answered Bowen.

'Oh, I'm sorry, but I'm not asking her. I'm telling her. She *has* to come,' shouted Einon.

'My sword says she doesn't have to,' said Bowen, and he pulled out his sword.

Einon smiled and pulled out his sword too. Then the teacher and his student started to fight. They fell down but quickly stood up again in the river. They looked strong and dangerous with their swords in their hands. But Einon was younger and faster.

Then the teacher and his student started to fight.

'Fight me, Bowen,' he called. 'You're a Knight of the Old Code. But nobody remembers the Old Code now. You're dead!'

His words made Bowen angrier. '*You* remember the Old Code! It's your Code too, you know,' he shouted.

'Never! It was never my Code,' Einon shouted back.

'Yes, it was. You repeated the words of the Old Code to the dragon in the mountain,' said Bowen.

'I only said those words because you wanted to hear them,' laughed Einon. 'And I wanted to live. You taught me to fight and you taught me well, Old Knight!' Then Einon brought his sword down hard on Bowen's arm. The knight fell down in the water.

But before Einon could kill Bowen, Draco came out of the river opposite him. The Great Dragon stood above the king and looked down at him with his angry, yellow eyes. Then Draco put

Then Draco put up his arms, and Einon saw the red light on his heart.

up his arms, and Einon saw the red light on his heart. The king felt very afraid. He climbed out of the river fast and jumped on to his horse. Kara, Bowen and Draco watched him, and Einon rode away.

Kara helped Bowen out of the river. She sat near him on the ground and washed his arm. 'You're a very strong fighter,' she said. 'Will you help the men in my village to fight Einon and his knights?'

'You won't win,' said Bowen. 'Einon will kill you.'

Kara looked at him angrily, then stood up. 'Will you fight with us, Draco?' she asked the dragon.

Draco looked at her sadly. 'For thousands of years dragons helped people. There was one dragon – the greatest dragon in the world. He told the other dragons to help the people in this country. Can you see that star up there? When the old dragon died that star was born. And after that, when other dragons died, new stars were born in the night sky. But then men stopped listening to the dragons. I wanted to do one wonderful thing for the people in this country. I wanted to be a star in the sky too. But I made a bad mistake. I helped to make the world a worse place . . .'

Bowen listened to the dragon's sad words. 'It was you!' he suddenly shouted. 'You're the dragon in the mountain. King Einon has half *your* heart!'

'Yes,' said Draco quietly. 'Einon will only die when I die. He's got half my heart. I wanted to help him. I wanted him to be good. But my heart didn't change him. I was stupid!'

'No you weren't,' said Bowen kindly. 'I wanted to help Einon too. I wanted to teach him the Old Code. But I couldn't.'

Then Draco turned to Kara. 'Yes, I'll fight Einon with you Kara,' he said. 'I'd like to help you. Come with us, Bowen.'

The knight thought for a minute. Then he stood up, and they all started to walk back to Kara's village.

When they arrived there, Kara asked the villagers to help her. She wanted them to fight Einon and kill him. But the men were angry and afraid. They shouted at her and began to hit her again.

Suddenly somebody said, 'Well, *I'm* going to fight Einon.' The men looked round. There, on his horse in the morning sun, was Sir Bowen. He had fire in his eyes and a smile on his face.

'Only you, Knight?' shouted the men.

'And Draco,' said Bowen. From behind a bridge Draco flew down to the village. The men looked at Bowen and then at Draco.

One of them shouted, 'I'm going to fight too. I want to fight Einon with this knight and the dragon.'

The other villagers listened and then they started to shout too, 'Kill Einon! Kill the cruel king! We want to fight!'

◆

For weeks everybody in the village got ready for the battle. On the last night the villagers gave Bowen a beautiful new sword. It shone in the firelight. On it was a picture of Draco – the dragon looked wonderful. Bowen couldn't say anything. He stood in the middle of the village and looked at the men round him. Then he looked at Draco and Kara and saw the love in his friends' eyes.

'You're ready for battle tomorrow,' he said to everybody. 'And you're ready to win. To win back your country. And the greatest dragon in the world is going to help you!'

Chapter 10 A New Star in the Sky

It was the day of the great battle. King Einon and his knights looked out of the castle windows.

'There are hundreds of peasants down there!' called Brok. 'They're ready to fight!'

'Then let's go!' answered Sir Felton. 'One of us is as strong as a hundred of them!'

'Don't be stupid!' Einon shouted at him. 'They've got Sir Bowen with them. And the dragon.'

Queen Aislinn came into the room. 'Don't be afraid of the dragon, my son,' she said quietly to Einon.

Einon turned to her. 'I'm not afraid of anything!' he said. 'But it's strange, you know, mother. Sometimes the dragon feels very near me.'

'Come with me, son,' said the queen, and walked out of the room.

Einon followed and saw five great, strong knights outside.

'These men are for you, my son. They're the strongest in the world,' the queen said.

'The strongest what?' Einon asked.

The fire from the dragon's nose burnt the king's buildings and men.

Einon, on his great white horse, pulled out his father's sword.

'The strongest dragon killers,' answered his mother.

Einon took his mother's hand. He looked into her eyes and thanked her warmly.

The king then went back to his knights. Below them they could see Bowen and the peasants. 'Look at them!' shouted Einon angrily. 'They're at my castle walls! Well, today Bowen's going to die, and the Old Code will die with him!'

Bowen rode up and down outside the castle, and looked up at Einon. 'Come down and fight,' he shouted. Einon heard him and felt very angry.

Suddenly Draco flew down into the castle. The fire from the dragon's nose burnt the king's buildings and men.

Einon watched and shouted, 'We can't stay here! We'll all burn. Let's go outside and fight those stupid peasants!'

He and his knights quickly ran down the stairs. They jumped on their horses and rode out of the castle. Einon, on his great white horse, pulled out his father's sword. 'Right! Let's kill them,' he shouted to his men.

Bowen saw Einon and shouted to the peasants, 'Quickly! Run! Run into the trees!' Einon and his knights followed the peasants but Bowen rode away from them.

The king and his men looked for the peasants in the trees. They didn't know that Bowen and hundreds of other peasants were behind them. Suddenly Bowen shouted out, 'Now!', and the peasants began to fight. They threw burning wood down on to Einon's men from behind them. Then hundreds of peasants came out of the trees in front of them too.

'Quickly! Back to the castle, or we'll die!' shouted Einon. He rode through the fire on his horse and his men followed. Bowen was near the king. He pulled out his sword and jumped on to Einon's horse. Then he pushed the sword through Einon's heart. But the king didn't stop. He didn't feel the sword!

At the same time, Draco suddenly fell from the sky into the

Suddenly Bowen shouted out, 'Now!', and the peasants began to fight.

castle. Bowen watched and shouted, 'No! Draco!' He thought about the dragon's words: 'Einon will only die when I die.'

He turned to Kara and said, 'Einon didn't feel my sword in his heart, but Draco felt it. Quickly! Let's go and help him.' Then he and Kara rode to the castle.

Einon also watched Draco fall from the sky. He saw his five dragon killers jump on to the dragon and pull out their swords. 'Stop,' he shouted. 'Don't kill him. I don't want the dragon to die. I want him to live. Then I'll never die.'

'No!' Draco cried. 'Kill me! Please!'

From a window in the castle the queen looked down at the dragon. She wanted to help him. She ran down the stairs with a knife in her hands.

'Come here, Aislinn,' Draco said, when he saw her.

'I've come to help you, Draco,' she said sadly. 'I've got a knife. I'm going to kill you.'

'I know,' said Draco. 'You *have* to kill me. Then cruel Einon will die. Are the stars shining in the sky tonight, Aislinn?'

'Yes, Great Dragon. They're beautiful,' answered the queen.

'Then kill me now,' said Draco.

But before the queen could do anything, somebody pulled the knife out of her hands. It was Einon. 'So, mother, you gave me the five dragon killers because you wanted them to kill this dragon,' he shouted angrily. 'You wanted him to die. And you wanted me to die too!'

'Yes, son. I made a mistake when you were a child. I asked the Great Dragon to help you. But now you're king, you're as cruel as your father. You have to die.'

Draco listened to the words of mother and son. He couldn't stop Einon. And he couldn't help the queen.

Bowen and Kara ran quickly into the castle and found Draco. 'Don't try to help me,' said the dragon. 'I'm tired and I want to die. Then Einon will die too.'

'But we won the battle!' shouted Bowen.

'You'll never win,' answered Draco. 'Kill me! Then you'll kill cruel King Einon. *Then* you'll win.'

'No, I can't,' cried Bowen. 'I can't kill you, dear Draco. You're the last dragon in the world.'

'This is the end for me, Bowen! Kill me!' said Draco.

'But you're my friend,' Bowen said.

'So kill me!' Draco shouted.

Suddenly Einon arrived and Bowen pulled out his sword. He tried to push the sword into the cruel king's heart, but Einon moved away quickly. By mistake Bowen's sword flew into Draco's heart! Bowen ran to the dragon and pulled it out. Then he turned and pushed it into Einon's heart. The king fell to the

Suddenly they saw a new star in the sky. It was Draco.

ground next to Draco. His eyes closed – cruel King Einon was dead.

Draco looked at Bowen and smiled warmly. Then he closed his eyes. Bowen went down on the ground near his friend.

'Are you going to leave us now, Draco? What will we do without you?'

Draco answered, 'I'm going up to the stars, dear Bowen. To my old dragon friends in the stars . . .'

In front of their eyes the dragon changed to starlight. Then Bowen and Kara watched the dragon's light fly up into the sky, to the other dragon stars. For a minute they couldn't see him, but suddenly they saw a new star in the sky. It was Draco.

'Look, Kara!' said Bowen. 'Look at Draco now. He's the biggest and most beautiful star in the sky!'

ACTIVITIES

Chapters 1–3

Before you read

1 Do you think that dragons really lived? When? Where?
Do you know any stories about dragons?

2 Find the words in *italics* in your dictionary. They are all in the story.

  a Put these words in the table:

    castle   dragon   field   king   knight   peasant   prince
    queen

    What other words can you put in the table?

Person	Animal	Place

  b Answer these questions.

    – What happens in a *battle*?

    – What can you carry in a *bucket*?

    – What can you *ride*?

    – Where can you see a *star*?

  c Look at the pictures on pages 1 and 6. Find these things in the
    pictures:

    beard   crown   sword

  d Are these sentences right?

    – When you die, your *heart* stops.

    – Mothers are usually *cruel* to their children.

    – When wood is dry, it *burns* easily.

    – People round the world live by the same *code*.

After you read

3 Who are these people? What do you know about them?

   a Sir Bowen   **d** Redbeard

   b Prince Einon   **e** Kara

   c King Freyne   **f** Queen Aislinn

4 Why does Sir Bowen think the Old Code is important? Why does the dragon want Einon to remember the Code?

Chapters 4–6

Before you read

5 When he is king, Einon doesn't remember the dragon's words. Why do you think he forgets the Old Code? What do you think he is going to do to the peasants?

6 Find the word *monk* in your dictionary. How are monks' lives different from other people's lives?

After you read

7 Who is speaking? Who to? Why do they say this?

   a 'Yes, I killed your father, boy! You can thank me now.'

   b 'I'm going to find that dragon ... and kill him!'

   c 'I don't want to fight. I've got an idea. Listen.'

8 Work with another student. Have a conversation.

   Student A: You are Sir Bowen, in the dragon's mouth. How do you feel? What would you like to happen? Tell the dragon.

   Student B: You are the dragon. Answer Sir Bowen.

9 Sir Bowen took Sir Felton's money.

   a Do you think he was right when he did this? Why/why not?

   b Why doesn't Sir Bowen live by the Old Code now?

Chapters 7–10

Before you read

10 How can Bowen and the dragon help the peasants? Can they fight cruel King Einon? Do you think they can win? How?

After you read

11 How do these people feel? Why?

    a Kara, about Einon; Einon, about Kara

    b Queen Aislinn, about Einon; Einon, about the queen

    c Kara, about Draco; Draco, about Kara

    d Sir Bowen, about Draco; Draco, about the knight

12 Why do the men in the village give Kara to the dragon? How do the villagers change in Chapter 9?

13 Draco wants to die in Chapter 10. And the queen, his friend, wants to kill him. Why?

Writing

14 Sir Bowen and Einon have very different ideas about the Old Code. Write about their ideas. Who do *you* think is right?

15 You are the monk, Brother Gilbert. You watch the fight between Bowen and the dragon. Write a story about the fight. How do you feel about it?

16 You are Queen Aislinn. You want your son, Einon, to die. Write a letter to him. Why do you want him to die? Why did you help Kara and the dragon?

17 It is a year after the story ends. You are Sir Bowen. Write about the country and the people in the story now. Who is king? Where is Kara? What are the peasants doing? Are people living by the Old Code?